Weight Watchers Smart Points Cookbook

Ultimate Collection of Weight Watchers Smart Points Recipes to Lose Weight and Get Fit – Nutrition Facts and Smart Points for Every Recipe!

By: Mikayla Sage

Weight Watchers Smart Points Cookbook

Legal notice

This book is copyright (c) 2017 by Mikayla Sage. All rights reserved. This book may not be copied or duplicated in whole or in part via any means including electronic forms of duplication such as audio or video recording or transcription. The contents of this book may not be stored in any retrieval system, transmitted, or otherwise copied for any use whether public or private, other than brief quotations contained in articles or reviews which fall under the "fair use" exception, without express prior permission of the publisher.

This book provides information only. The author does not offer any advice, medical or otherwise, or suggest a particular course of action in any specific situation, nor is this book meant as a substitute for any professional advice, medical or otherwise. The reader accepts all responsibility for how he or she chooses to use the information contained in this book and under no circumstances will the author or publisher be held liable for any damages caused directly or indirectly by any information contained in this book.

Weight Watchers Smart Points Cookbook

Table of Contents

INTRODUCTION 8

What is Weight Watchers? 8

How do Smart Points work? 10

How do Smart Points differ from other counting methods? 10

SOUP RECIPES 15

White Bean & Winter Squash Stew 16

Asian Chicken Soup 18

Garlic Flavored Sprouts Soup 21

Mixed Veggie and Beans Soup 23

Spicy Plum Tomato Soup 26

Slow Cooked Artichoke Soup 29

Yummy Sweet Potato Soup 32

Clam Chowder 34

Tasty Tomato and Carrot Soup 37

VEGETARIAN RECIPES 41

Delicious Cauliflower Tabouli 42

Grilled Tofu Avocado Wrap 44

Fruit and Nut Spinach Salad 46

Mint and Cucumber Salad 47

Quinoa and Kale Salad 49

Olive & Peas Orzo Salad 51

Delicious Eggplant Adobo 53

Thai Tempeh Bowl 55

Weight Watchers Smart Points Cookbook

Delicious Marinated Eggplant 57
Quinoa with Veggies & Chickpeas 59
   CHICKEN RECIPES 63
Chicken Tomato in Red 64
Simple Grilled Bruschetta 67
Broccoli-Chicken Zucchini Boats 70
Spinach Chicken Salads 73
Slow-Cooker BBQ Chicken 76
Roasted Chicken with Asparagus 79
Chicken Satay 82
Easy Paprika Chicken 85
   FISH RECIPES 89
Baked Crispy Salmon 90
Walnut-Crusted Baked Salmon Fillets 93
Roasted Tomato Salmon 95
Lean and Healthy Baked Cod 98
Salmon Salads with Asparagus 101
Spicy Tuna Salad 104
Salmon Poke Bowl 106
Salmon with Mushroom and Spinach 109
Cucumber Sushi Rolls 111
Simple Lemon Wild Salmon 114
   BEEF RECIPES 117
Beef Steak in Tomato Sauce 118

Weight Watchers Smart Points Cookbook

Beef Patty Cucumber Salad 121
Brown Beef Potato Stew 125
Spiced Beef Stew with Carrots and Blueberries 128
Korean Beef-Stuffed Peppers 131
Spicy Beef and Butternut Squash Stew 134
Sautéed Beef Onion 137
    PORK RECIPES 141
Delicious Pork with Sour Strawberry Sauce 142
Tasty Pork Meatballs in Tomato Sauce 145
Sunflower-Butter Pork Kabobs 148
Delicious Pork in Blanket 151
Pork Chops w/ a Cumin Crust 153
Spicy Pork Ribs 156
    DESSERT RECIPES 161
Refreshing Mango Ice Cream 162
Creamy Cherry Sorbet 164
Oat Banana Cookies 166
Almond Mango Mint Popsicles 168
Orange Peach Popsicles 170
Mango Silk Pudding 172
No Crust Pumpkin Cheesecake 174
Fruit Pastry Tart 176
Apricot Rice Pudding 178
Simple Apple Dip 180

Weight Watchers Smart Points Cookbook

INTRODUCTION

Obesity in the United States is becoming increasingly problematic, and consequently, people are informing themselves of the ways in which obesity negatively impacts health. Many turn to trending, fad diets, which all promise fast and amazing results. Though diets like these have come and gone, few have consistently proven as successful as Weight Watchers, which boasts a community of millions of healthy and improved lives.

This book seeks build a clear understanding of the Weight Watchers diet, and explain how counting "Smart Points" of different foods can contribute to both weight loss, and an overall healthier, happier life.

What is Weight Watchers?

Weight Watchers takes pride in its scientifically founded weight loss diet. Instead of making broad generalizations and condemning entire food groups, Weight Watchers assigns Smart Points to the foods that you already consume. Rather than dictating foods that you either can or cannot eat, the diet operates under the philosophy that by counting Smart Points and staying within a healthy point range, your weight will come down. In addition, Weight Watchers believes that the diet is only one aspect of long-term weight management. Healthy bodies are the result of a healthy lifestyle, which include a person's mental, emotional, and physical wellbeing. The diet's primary focus on long-term weight management warns against quick and unhealthy weight loss, which is often gained back as quickly as it was lost. So, while you might see celebrities turning to cayenne and lemon, or buying into expensive juice cleanses, do not be tempted into following the fads. These diets are neither feasible, nor practical for the average person, even if they do offer short-term results.

Weight Watchers was founded by Jean Nidetch in the 60s, when she started hosting weekly discussions on weight-loss methods at her home in Queens, NY. At first, the group consisted of only a handful of friends, but today, Weight Watchers has grown to include millions of members around the globe.

Early marketing strategies were primarily focused towards women in early advertisement campaigns, but men began to use Weight Watchers after witnessing its success — even professional athletes. Charles Barkley, a former NBA basketball player, testified to losing 42 pounds on Weight Watchers.

Before getting started, Weight Watchers lists a few health factors that limit eligibility. To be eligible for Weight Watchers, you must NOT:

- Be 5 pounds within the minimum healthy weight according to your height, per the Weight Watchers Healthy Weight Ranges.
- Be pregnant or expecting child.
- Be diagnosed with *bulimia nervosa*.

How do Smart Points work?

Smart Point values are assigned to food items based on factors that directly affect weight gain. Primary factors typically include calories and macro-nutrients. Smart Points increase as the amount of saturated fats and sugars in the food increase. Conversely, the presence of lean proteins and nutrient-dense carbohydrates will decrease a food's Smart Points value. Essentially, there are four main factors that give a food its Smart Points value: Proteins, sugars, saturated fat, and calories.

How do Smart Points differ from other counting methods?

Weight Watchers began its 1-2-3 Success Program in 1997. The points system created a simple way for practicing members to keep track of calories, fibers, and fat contents of the foods and beverages they regularly consumed.

The points program provides members with a target goal of Points allowed for each day. They were encouraged to keep track of the foods and beverages that they consumed so that they could stay under their target points and lose weight.

Weight Watchers' points-based program is widely embraced, and remains the driving force behind the program.

The program was slightly modified and renamed to Winning Points early in the 2000s. Under the new program, members became able to gain additional points for logging daily exercise. The additional points could then be factored in with the consumption of additional foods and beverages.

Another modification—named the Turn Around Program—replaced Winning Points shortly thereafter. In this program, members became able to choose one of two courses of action. The first option, the Core Program, was focused on selecting healthier foods from an allowed foods list, while avoiding items on a list of restricted foods. The second option, The Flex Plan, permitted dieters to consume anything they desired, but required them to track their food and beverage consumption. Dieters later calculated the points from the day, making sure to stay within their daily points allowance.

Weight Watchers did away with the Core Program in 2009, and replaced it with the Weight Watchers Momentum Plan. This plan instructed members to consume foods that filled them, allowing them to consume less foods overall, while also preventing overeating.

Weight Watchers replaced the Momentum Plan in 2012 by introducing the Points Plus program. This program was popular through December 2015, when Weight Watchers introduced Smart Points. The Smart Points program was quickly recognized as a superior points system, and brought a quick end to Points Plus.

Smart Points verses Points Plus

- The distinguishing factor between Smart Point values and Points Plus values concerns the way that macro-nutrient presence and calorie content in a food item changes its overall point value. Points Plus measured the levels of carbohydrates, fats, proteins and fibres were present in foods, while the Smart Point value places more emphasis on a food's proteins, sugars, saturated fats, and caloric content.

- Point Plus overemphasised calorie counting, excluding other critical factors in weight loss. Smart Points incorporated elements of an overall healthier lifestyle, basing healthy food choices on more than just caloric content.

- Points Plus could be "gamed," meaning that dieters could easily consume unhealthy foods on a regular basis while staying within the point allowance for healthy eating.

- The Smart Points system places much more emphasis on the consumption of vegetables and fruits than Points Plus did. These items typically have point values of zero in Smart Points.

- The Smart Point program incorporates a system of Fit Points, which are derived from all activities throughout the day.

Smart Points vs. Older Points Systems

Older point systems were based on an oversimplified "calories consumed" and "calories burned" understanding of dieting. They focused on decreasing dietary fat and increasing the intake of dietary fiber. Smart Points approaches dieting more holistically, and factors in a more complex understanding of the role that proteins, calories, sugars, and saturated fats have in weight management.

Weight Watchers Smart Points Cookbook

Weight Watchers Smart Points Cookbook

SOUP RECIPES

White Bean & Winter Squash Stew

SmartPoints: 5

Ingredients

1 pound dried navy beans (soaked overnight and drained)

Pinch of baking soda

1 onion (chopped)

5 cups water

4 garlic cloves (minced)

1 ½ teaspoon cumin (ground)

4 teaspoons smoked paprika

2 teaspoons oregano (dried)

½ teaspoon cumin (ground)

1 teaspoon basil (dried)

1 pound winter squash (peeled and cubed)

1 (15 oz) can diced tomatoes

1 bunch kale (stems discarded and chopped)

1 teaspoon sea salt

½ cup chopped fresh basil

Instructions:

- Heat a pressure cooker and add the onion and baking soda to it, sautéing for 3-4 minutes until the onion begins to brown.
- Add the garlic and stir fry for a minute
- Add the water, beans, dried basil, 1 teaspoon cumin and half the paprika and oregano to the pressure cooker, close and bring to high pressure.
- Cook for 8 minutes and then release the pressure.
- Mix in the squash with the rest of the ingredients except the kale and fresh basil and cook covered at high pressure for 8 additional minutes.
- Mix in the kale and cook covered until tender.
- Mix in the basil, cook for 1 minute and serve.

Makes: 6 servings

Nutritional information per serving:

Calories: 383; Total Fat: 2.3 g; Carbohydrates: 44.3 g; Proteins: 22 g

Asian Chicken Soup

SmartPoints: 6

Serving: 2

Nutrition Facts

Serving Size 499 g

Amount Per Serving

Calories 337

Calories from Fat 86

% Daily Value*

Total Fat 9.5g

15%

Saturated Fat 3.4g

17%

Trans Fat 0.0g

Cholesterol 132mg

44%

Sodium 855mg

36%

Potassium 291mg

8%

Total Carbohydrates 4.5g

1%

Dietary Fiber 0.9g

3%

Sugars 1.9g

Protein 56.0g

Vitamin A 47%   •   Vitamin C 5%

Calcium 2%   •   Iron 12%

Nutrition Grade C

Ingredients:

1 lb. skinless, boneless chicken breast

2 tablespoons chopped onion

1 teaspoon minced garlic

½ teaspoon ginger powder

¼ cup chopped carrot

¼ cup chopped yellow sweet potato

2 tablespoons chopped green beans

2 cups vegetable broth

½ teaspoon pepper

¼ teaspoon salt

Directions:

- Chop the chicken then place it in a Dutch oven together with vegetable broth.
- Bring to boil and once it is boiled, add onion, minced garlic, and ginger powder into the Dutch oven.
- Cover with the lid and cook for approximately 15 minutes.
- When it is done, open the lid then add chopped carrot and sweet potato into the soup then bring to a simmer for another 15 minutes.
- Season with salt and pepper then transfer to a soup bowl.
- Serve and enjoy hot.

Garlic Flavored Sprouts Soup

SmartPoints: 2

Ingredients

1 tablespoon garlic (chopped)

2 cups sprouted whole green gram

1 cup shredded spinach

Salt to taste

3 cups water

Instructions:

- Combine the garlic, 3 cups water and green grams in a pressure cooker and cook until 2 whistles are heard.
- Release the steam.
- Using an immersion blender, blend the mixture.
- Transfer the mixture into a non-stick skillet and add the spinach, 1 cup water and salt.
- Stir well and cook for around 5 minutes, stirring occasionally.

Makes: 4 servings

Nutritional information per serving:

Calories: 95 kcal ; Total Fat: 0.5 g; Carbohydrates: 15.8 g; Proteins: 6.8 g

Weight Watchers Smart Points Cookbook

Mixed Veggie and Beans Soup

SmartPoints: 2

Serving: 8

Nutrition Facts

Serving Size 138 g

Amount Per Serving

Calories 69

Calories from Fat 19

% Daily Value*

Total Fat 2.2g

3%

Trans Fat 0.0g

Cholesterol 0mg

0%

Sodium 103mg

4%

Potassium 278mg

8%

Total Carbohydrates 9.5g

Weight Watchers Smart Points Cookbook

3%

Dietary Fiber 2.5g

10%

Sugars 1.3g

Protein 3.7g

* Based on a 2000 calorie diet

Nutrition Facts

Ingredients:

3 teaspoons olive oil

¼ cup chopped onion

¼ cup chopped carrots

1 teaspoon minced garlic

¼ cup chopped broccoli

1 cup vegetable broth

2 cups water

1 cup diced tomatoes

½ cup kidney beans

2 tablespoons sliced zucchini

3 teaspoons oregano

¼ teaspoon pepper

Directions:

- Place a Dutch oven over medium heat then pour olive oil in it.
- Once the oil is hot, stir in chopped onion, carrots, and garlic then sauté until aromatic.
- Pour vegetable broth and water over the sautéed ingredients then bring to boils.
- Once it is boiled, add the remaining ingredient, stir well then cover.
- Bring to a simmer for approximately 20 minutes
- Transfer the soup into a serving bowl then serve hot.

Spicy Plum Tomato Soup

SmartPoints: 5

Serves: 6

Time: 1 hour, 20 minutes

Ingredients:

3 pounds of plum tomatoes

1 quart of chicken broth

6 garlic cloves

1 sweet onion

½ cup basil

3 tablespoons olive oil

2 tablespoons butter

2 tablespoons tomato paste

1 tablespoon salt

1 tablespoon sriracha

1 teaspoon crushed red pepper

½ teaspoon thyme

½ teaspoon pepper

½ teaspoon paprika

Directions:

1. Divide up the plum tomatoes into thirds.

2. Wash and dry ⅓ of the tomatoes and cut them in half, lengthwise.

3. Grease a baking sheet and arrange the cut tomatoes with the cut-side up.

4. Season with olive oil and salt.

5. Bake at 400-degrees for 40 minutes.

6. In the meantime, cut the onion and put the garlic through a garlic press.

7. Pour 1 tablespoon of olive oil in a large pot and cook the garlic and onion until translucent.

8. Cut the rest of the tomatoes into chunks (the fresh ones) and add them to the pot.

9. Pour in the broth and bring to a boil.

10. Toss in the basil leaves, along with butter and tomato paste.

11. Add the spices.

12. Bring to a boil on the stove.

13. When the tomatoes in the oven are roasted, put them in the pot and reduce the heat to a simmer.

14. After 40 minutes, pour into a large blender and process until creamy.

15. Pour into bowls and serve!

Nutritional Info:

Total calories: 164

Carbs: 9

Fat: 12

Protein: 3

Fiber: 2.7

Slow Cooked Artichoke Soup

SmartPoints: 6

Ingredients

Cashew Cheese:

½ cup pieces of raw cashew (placed in ½ cup low-sodium vegetable broth)

½ tablespoon nutritional yeast

½ lemon juice

½ teaspoon garlic powder

Soy Curls:

½ cup soy curls (placed in hot water for 15 minutes)

2 tablespoons water

1 garlic clove (chopped)

1 teaspoon sage (rubbed)

1 teaspoon garlic powder

½ teaspoon sweet paprika

½ teaspoon oregano (dried)

¼ teaspoon black pepper

½ teaspoon fennel seeds

Pinch of sea salt

1 tablespoon dry red wine

Soup:

1 onion (chopped)

1 carrot (chopped)

4 garlic cloves (minced)

2 celery stalks (chopped)

½ teaspoon fennel seeds

½ teaspoon rosemary (dried)

½ teaspoon oregano (dried)

½ teaspoon garlic powder

½ teaspoon thyme (dried)

Dash of sea salt, black pepper and red pepper flakes

5 ½ cups low-sodium vegetable broth

4 (4-ounce) cans artichoke hearts (drained and chopped)

Instructions:

- For the cashew cheese, combine all the cashew cheese ingredients in a blender and process until smooth.

- For cooking the soy curls, first combine the soy curl ingredients except the red wine in a saucepan and cook until it begins to brown. Deglaze the pan using the wine.
- For the soup, heat a skillet, add 2 tablespoon water and sauté the carrots, onions and celery in it for 5 minutes. Add the herbs, spices and garlic and cook for another minute. Transfer the ingredients into a slow cooker.
- Add 5 cups of the broth and the artichoke hearts to the slow cooker and cook for 8 hours on low.
- Using an immersion blender, blend the soup in the slow cooker.
- Stir the soy curls into the soup and garnish it with the cashew cheese.

Makes: 6 servings

Nutritional information per serving:

Calories: 219; Total Fat: 7 g; Carbohydrates: 35 g; Proteins: 11 g

Yummy Sweet Potato Soup

SmartPoints: 9

Total Time: 35 minutes

Serves: 4 Servings

Ingredients:

- 1 lb sweet potatoes, peeled and diced
- 3/4 cup cream
- 2 garlic clove, minced
- 2 onions, chopped
- 10 oz carrots, peeled and diced
- 4 cups vegetable stock
- 3 tbsp olive oil
- Pepper
- Salt

Directions:

1. Heat oven at 200 F.
2. Place carrots and sweet potatoes onto the roasting tray and drizzle with 2 tbsp olive oil and season with pepper and salt.
3. Place tray in oven and roast for 25 minutes.
4. In a sauce pan, add 1 tablespoon olive oil over the medium-high heat.
5. Add onion in pan sauté for 10 minutes then add garlic and vegetable stock.
6. Remove roasted vegetables from oven and let it cool for 5 minutes.
7. Add roasted vegetables in sauce pan and blend it with blender until get smooth mixture. Stir cream.
8. Serve hot and enjoy.

Nutritional Value (Amount per Serving):

- Calories 305
- Fat 13.5 g
- Carbohydrates 44.9 g
- Sugar 7.3 g
- Protein 3.4 g
- Cholesterol 8 mg

Clam Chowder

SmartPoints: 10

Serves: 4

Time: 45 minutes

Ingredients:

½ head cauliflower

16-ounces of canned clams

2 ½ cups heavy cream

1 cup water

1 cup clam juice

3 strips bacon

4 garlic cloves

2 celery stalks

1 carrot

1 onion

2 tablespoons butter

1 teaspoon xanthan gum

1 teaspoon salt

1 teaspoon parsley

½ teaspoon thyme

½ teaspoon pepper

½ teaspoon celery salt

Directions:

1. Fill a pot with water to boil the cauliflower and heat.

2. When it's hot, chop up the cauliflower and put it in the pot to cook for 10 minutes until very soft.

3. In the meantime, cube the bacon and mince the onions and carrots.

4. Cut the celery into ¼-inch slices.

5. In a separate pot, cook the bacon until it's almost crispy, then add the onion, carrot, and celery.

6. Season with a little salt and cook until the onion is turning clear.

7. Add the garlic and butter.

8. Separate the canned clams and juice, saving the juice.

9. Drain the cauliflower and process in a blender until smooth.

10. Add the cauliflower, water, clam juice, and heavy cream into the bacon/veggies pot.

11. Reduce the heat and simmer for 20 minutes.

12. Season.

13. Add the xanthan gum and mix.

14. Add the clams and cook for just 5 minutes to avoid tough clams.

15. Serve!

Nutritional Info:

Total calories: 404

Carbs: 15

Fat: 38

Protein: 28

Fiber: 0

Weight Watchers Smart Points Cookbook

Tasty Tomato and Carrot Soup

SmartPoints: 4

Total Time: 1 hour 20 minutes

Serves: 8 Servings

Ingredients:

- 1 carrot, peeled and cut into small pieces
- 2 potato, peeled and diced
- 1 cup coriander, chopped
- 2 garlic clove, minced
- 1 tbsp ginger, grated
- 1 onion, chopped
- 2 tomatoes, chopped
- 4 tbsp olive oil
- 1 tsp pepper
- 1 tsp cumin

- 5 cups water
- 2 tsp salt

Directions:

1. In a saucepan heat olive oil over medium heat.
2. Add onion, ginger, garlic and carrots in pan and sauté for 5 minutes over medium heat.
3. Add tomatoes, potatoes and chopped coriander sauté for further 5 minutes.
4. Add remaining ingredients and bring to boil.
5. Cover pan with lid and simmer over medium-low heat for 60 minutes. Add more water if necessary.
6. Puree soup with blender until completely smooth.
7. Serve hot and enjoy.

Nutritional Value (Amount per Serving):

- Calories 125
- Fat 7.3 g
- Carbohydrates 14.7 g
- Sugar 2.9 g
- Protein 2 g
- Cholesterol 0 mg

Weight Watchers Smart Points Cookbook

VEGETARIAN RECIPES

Delicious Cauliflower Tabouli

SmartPoints: 6

Total Time: 15 minutes

Serves: 4 Servings

Ingredients:

- 1/2 head of cauliflower, cut into florets
- 1 cucumber, peeled and diced
- 1 bunch green onions, chopped
- 2 cups tomatoes, diced
- 3 bunch parsley, chopped
- 2 tbsp fresh mint, chopped
- 3 tbsp fresh lemon juice
- 1/3 cup extra virgin olive oil
- 1/4 tsp ground black pepper
- 1/2 tsp sea salt

Directions:

1. Place cauliflower florets into the food processor. Pulse until get couscous consistency.
2. Transfer cauliflower mixture into the large mixing bowl.
3. Add cucumber, green onion, tomatoes, parsley, mint, lemon juice and olive oil. Toss well to combine.
4. Season with pepper and salt to taste.
5. Serve immediately and enjoy.

Nutritional Value (Amount per Serving):

- Calories 184
- Fat 17.2 g
- Carbohydrates 8.6 g
- Sugar 4.7 g
- Protein 2.1 g
- Cholesterol 0 mg

Grilled Tofu Avocado Wrap

SmartPoints: 6

Total Time: 20 minutes

Serves: 4 Servings

Ingredients:

- 1 block extra firm tofu, drained
- 1 avocado, peeled and sliced
- 4 large flour tortillas
- 1 red bell pepper, sliced
- 1 onion, sliced
- 1/2 tsp cayenne pepper
- 2 tbsp canola oil
- 2 tbsp Montreal steak seasoning
- Honey mustard

Directions:

1. Preheat the grill.
2. In a bowl, combine together Montreal steak seasoning, cayenne and canola oil.
3. Cut tofu into 1 inch slices and dip into the seasoning mixture then place on hot grill.
4. Grilled tofu for 5 minutes.
5. Toss bell pepper and onion and remaining seasoning mixture, and grill until charred.
6. Place tortilla on hot grill for 30 seconds, flip once to toast each side.
7. Place tortillas on separate plates and spread with honey mustard.
8. Assemble wrap by dividing grilled tofu, avocado and grilled vegetables among the tortillas.
9. Wrap tightly and serve.

Nutritional Value (Amount per Serving):

- Calories 186
- Fat 16.9 g
- Carbohydrates 9.3 g
- Sugar 2.9 g
- Protein 1.6 g
- Cholesterol 0 mg

Fruit and Nut Spinach Salad

SmartPoints: 3

Ingredients

5 oz Baby spinach (fresh)

1 oz pine nuts

¼ cup golden raisins

½ tart sweet apple (cored, chopped)

¼ cup vegetable broth

2 tablespoons of fresh lemon juice

Instructions:

- Combine the apple, raisins and pine nuts in a skillet and lightly brown it, stirring often.
- Pour in the broth and add the spinach, leaving to wilt.
- Remove from the flame and mix in the lemon juice.
- Toss all the ingredients together.

Makes: 4 servings

Nutritional information per serving:

Calories: 95; Total Fat: 5 g; Carbohydrates: 13 g; Proteins: 2 g

Mint and Cucumber Salad

SmartPoints: 1

Total Time: 10 minutes

Serves: 2 Servings

Ingredients:

- 1 large English cucumber
- 1 tbsp chili sauce
- 1 tbsp extra virgin olive oil
- 1 tbsp sesame oil
- 2 tbsp rice wine vinegar
- 1 handful fresh mint leaves
- 1/2 onion

Directions:

1. Slice onion and cucumber thinly using knife or vegetable slicer.

2. In mixing bowl add together slice cucumber, onion and mint leaves.

3. In small bowl mix together chili sauce, olive oil, sesame oil and rice wine vinegar.

4. Just before serving add dressing and toss well.

5. Serve immediately and enjoy.

Nutritional Value (Amount per Serving):

- Calories 170
- Fat 14.1 g
- Carbohydrates 9.1 g
- Sugar 3.8 g
- Protein 1.7 g
- Cholesterol 0 mg

Quinoa and Kale Salad

SmartPoints: 9

Total Time: 20 minutes

Serves: 4 Servings

Ingredients:

- 1/2 quinoa, cooked
- 4 cups kale, chopped
- 1 lemon zest
- 3 tbsp fresh lemon juice
- 4 tbsp olive oil
- 4 tbsp apple cider vinegar
- 1/2 cup almonds, sliced
- 1/2 cup pomegranate seeds
- 1 avocado, diced

- 2 tbsp pecans, chopped
- Black pepper
- 1 tsp sea salt

Directions:

1. In small bowl, whisk together lemon zest, lemon juice, apple cider vinegar and olive oil. Set aside.
2. In large mixing bowl, add kale, quinoa, avocado, pecans and pomegranate. Mix well.
3. Pour dressing on top of salad and toss well to combine.
4. Season with pepper and salt to taste.
5. Serve immediately and enjoy.

Nutritional Value (Amount per Serving):

- Calories 462
- Fat 16.1 g
- Carbohydrates 44.7 g
- Sugar 10.4 g
- Protein 19.1 g
- Cholesterol 0 mg

Olive & Peas Orzo Salad

SmartPoints: 11

Ingredients

¾ cups whole-wheat orzo

1 tomato (chopped)

1 (15 oz) can black eyed peas (drained and rinsed)

2 tablespoons fresh parsley (chopped)

2 tablespoons red wine vinegar

2 tablespoons orange juice

2 garlic cloves (minced)

½ English cucumber (cored, diced)

½ cup Kalamata olives, pitted (chopped)

1/3 cup red onions (chopped)

1 teaspoon lemon zest

2 tablespoons lemon juice

2 tablespoons vegetable broth

1 teaspoon dried oregano

¼ cup pepperoncini (chopped)

Sea salt and pepper to taste

Instructions:

- Cook the orzo pasta as per the packet instructions and place aside.
- Mix together the peas, parsley, tomato, red wine vinegar, garlic, and orange juice in a bowl and mix well. Season it with a pinch of sea salt and pepper and leave aside for 15 minutes.
- Combine all the ingredients including the cooked orzo and peas mixture in a salad bowl and toss to mix.

Makes: 4 servings

Nutritional information per serving:

Calories: 445; Total Fat: 4 g; Carbohydrates: 79 g; Proteins: 28 g

Delicious Eggplant Adobo

SmartPoints: 15

Total Time: 25 minutes

Serves: 4 Servings

Ingredients:

- 5 medium eggplants, ends trimmed
- 1 tsp sugar
- 5 garlic cloves, chopped
- 4 tbsp soy sauce
- 1/4 tsp ground pepper
- 1/3 cup vinegar
- 1/2 cup vegetable oil

Directions:

1. Cut eggplant in half lengthwise and then cut each half into 2 inch pieces.
2. Heat vegetable oil in frying pan over medium-high heat.

3. Once oil is hot then fry eggplant in batches and drain on paper towel. Set aside.

4. Take another pan and add soy sauce, vinegar, sugar, garlic and ground pepper. Bring to boil.

5. Add fried eggplant into the pan and stir well.

6. Cover pan with lid and cook for 3 minutes or until eggplants are soft.

7. Serve hot with rice and enjoy.

Nutritional Value (Amount per Serving):

- Calories 434
- Fat 28.5 g
- Carbohydrates 44.0 g
- Sugar 21.9 g
- Protein 8.0 g
- Cholesterol 0 mg

Thai Tempeh Bowl

SmartPoints: 6

Ingredients

2 cups mixed greens

1/3 container tempeh (seasoned and cooked)

1/3 cup quinoa (cooked)

¼ cup red bell pepper (chopped)

¼ cup purple cabbage (shredded)

¼ cup sweet potato (roasted, chopped)

¼ cup chopped avocado

Cashew curry:

1 tablespoon coconut milk

1 tablespoon cashew butter

½ tablespoon low-sodium soy sauce

½ teaspoon red curry paste

1 teaspoon rice vinegar

Instructions:

- For the sauce, combine all the curry ingredients in a bowl and whisk vigorously.
- Toss together the tempeh, quinoa and greens in a bowl.
- Layer the vegetables along the edges of the bowl and top with the cashew curry.

Makes: 1 serving

Nutritional information per serving:

Calories: 275; Total Fat: 10 g; Carbohydrates: 40 g; Proteins: 20 g

Delicious Marinated Eggplant

SmartPoints: 9

Total Time: 2 hours

Serves: 4 Servings

Ingredients:

- 18 oz eggplant, cut into slices
- 1 bell pepper, roasted and diced
- 3/4 cup olive oil, divided
- 1 tbsp parsley, chopped
- 1 garlic clove, minced
- 1 small jalapeno pepper, seeded and chopped
- 1/4 tsp pepper
- 1 tsp salt

Directions:

1. Place eggplant slices in plate and sprinkle with salt both the side. Brush the eggplant with oil. Set aside for 30 minutes.

2. In a pan, heat olive oil over the medium-high heat and place eggplant onto the pan cook both the side until golden brown.

3. Transfer the eggplant slices in bowl and add bell pepper, parsley, garlic, jalapeno, pepper and salt in bowl toss well until combined.

4. Cover the bowl with lid and marinate in refrigerator for 1 hour.

Nutritional Value (Amount per Serving):

- Calories 367
- Fat 28.1 g
- Carbohydrates 9.7 g
- Sugar 5.1 g
- Protein 1.6 g
- Cholesterol 0 mg

Quinoa with Veggies & Chickpeas

SmartPoints: 10

Ingredients

1 ½ cups quinoa (rinsed)

3 cups vegetable broth

2 garlic cloves (minced)

1 teaspoon sea salt

Veggie & Chickpea Mix:

4 garlic cloves (minced)

4 teaspoons cumin (ground)

1 teaspoon turmeric

2 teaspoons paprika (smoked)

½ teaspoon cardamom (ground)

¼ teaspoon cayenne pepper

4 cups cauliflower florets

1 eggplant (cubed)

2 (15 oz) can chickpeas (rinsed and drained)

2 (16oz) can diced tomatoes with juices

1 cup raisins

½ cup water

2 zucchinis (cubed)

Instructions:

- For the quinoa, heat a saucepan and toast the quinoa in it, stirring continuously. Pour in the broth and add the garlic and salt to it. Bring to boil, reduce the flame and cook for around 15-10 minutes till the water is absorbed. Fluff.
- Heat a skillet over medium flame, add 2 tablespoon water and sauté the onions in it Add the garlic, turmeric, cayenne, cardamom, paprika and cumin, stir cooking for 2 minutes.
- Add the rest of the ingredients to the skillet except the zucchini and cook covered for 10 minutes, stirring occasionally on low flame.
- Mix in the zucchini and cook covered for another 10 minutes.
- Serve the chickpea & veggie mix over the quinoa.

Makes: 8 servings

Nutritional information per serving:

Calories: 370; Total Fat: 3.8 g; Carbohydrates: 73.7 g; Proteins: 14 g

Weight Watchers Smart Points Cookbook

Weight Watchers Smart Points Cookbook

CHICKEN RECIPES

Weight Watchers Smart Points Cookbook

Chicken Tomato in Red

SmartPoints: 3

Serving: 2

Nutrition Facts

Serving Size 304 g

Amount Per Serving

Calories 66

Calories from Fat 5

% Daily Value*

Total Fat 0.6g

1%

Trans Fat 0.0g

Cholesterol 0mg

0%

Sodium 17mg

1%

Potassium 690mg

Weight Watchers Smart Points Cookbook

20%

Total Carbohydrates 14.7g

5%

Dietary Fiber 4.2g

17%

Sugars 8.3g

Protein 2.9g

Ingredients:

- 2 medium tomatoes
- ½ cup chopped chicken fillet without fat
- 1 medium turkey sausage without fat
- ¼ cup diced green pepper
- ¼ cup chopped onion
- 1 teaspoon minced garlic
- ¼ teaspoon black pepper
- 1 teaspoon chopped celery, for garnish

Directions:

- Stew the tomatoes until soft then let them cool for a few minutes.
- Place the chopped chicken fillet and stewed tomato in medium stockpot then cooks on high heat until the chicken is completely cooked.

- Cut the turkey sausage into slices then add into the cooked chicken together with green pepper, chopped onion, and minced garlic.
- Season with black pepper then stir until well combined.
- Bring to a simmer for approximately 20 minutes over medium heat.
- Once it is done, transfer the cooked chicken together with the remaining sauce to a serving dish.
- Sprinkle chopped celery over the chicken for garnish.
- Serve and enjoy warm.

Weight Watchers Smart Points Cookbook

Simple Grilled Bruschetta

SmartPoints: 6

Serving: 4

Nutrition Facts

Serving Size 92 g

Amount Per Serving

Calories 221

Calories from Fat 43

% Daily Value*

Total Fat 4.8g

7%

Saturated Fat 0.8g

4%

Cholesterol 0mg

0%

Sodium 418mg

17%

Potassium 147mg

4%

Total Carbohydrates 37.4g

12%

Dietary Fiber 2.0g

8%

Sugars 2.2g

Protein 7.8g

Vitamin A 5% • Vitamin C 8%

Calcium 3% • Iron 14%

Nutrition Grade A-

* Based on a 2000 calorie diet

Ingredients:

8 slices French bread

½ cup cooked chicken cubes

½ cup diced tomato

1 tablespoon chopped parsley

1-tablespoon olive oil

1 tablespoon crushed garlic

1-teaspoon black pepper

2 tablespoons mayonnaise

Directions:

- Combine chicken cubes, diced tomato, olive oil, and crushed garlic in a bowl then mix until well combined.

- Preheat an oven to 400 °F then lines a baking pan with aluminum foil.
- Brush each French bread slices with mayonnaise then put a spoonful of tomato chicken mixture on the top of each slice.
- Sprinkle black pepper and parsley on top then arrange the topped French bread on the prepared baking pan and bake for approximately 4 minutes.
- Remove from the oven and arrange on a serving platter.
- Serve and enjoy.

Broccoli-Chicken Zucchini Boats

SmartPoints: 10

Serves: 2

Time: About 35 minutes

Ingredients:

2 hollowed-out, big zucchinis

6 ounces of shredded chicken

3 ounces of shredded Cheddar cheese

1 cup of broccoli

1 green onion stalk

2 tablespoons butter

2 tablespoons sour cream

Salt and pepper to taste

Directions:

1. Preheat your oven to 400-degrees.

2. Cut the zucchini in half, lengthwise, and hollow out with a spoon so you get a shell that's about 1-centimeter thick.

3. Pour 1 tablespoon of melted butter into the zucchini, sprinkle on salt and pepper, and put in the oven for 20 minutes.

4. In the meantime, shred the chicken and cut up your broccoli.

5. Mix with the sour cream and add salt and pepper.

6. When 20 minutes is up, fill the boats with the chicken-broccoli filling.

7. Sprinkle on the cheddar cheese and bake until the cheese has melted, about 10-15 minutes.

8. Top with chopped green onion and serve!

Nutritional Info:

Total calories: 476

Carbs: 5

Fat: 24

Protein: 30

Fiber: 3

Weight Watchers Smart Points Cookbook

Spinach Chicken Salads

SmartPoints: 6

Serving: 2

Nutrition Facts

Serving Size 238 g

Amount Per Serving

Calories 257

Calories from Fat 130

% Daily Value*

Total Fat 14.4g

22%

Saturated Fat 2.9g

14%

Trans Fat 0.0g

Cholesterol 66mg

22%

Sodium 339mg

14%

Potassium 217mg

6%

Total Carbohydrates 2.9g

1%

Dietary Fiber 1.3g

5%

Sugars 0.7g

Protein 28.9g

Vitamin A 28%   •   Vitamin C 13%

Calcium 4%   •   Iron 9%

Nutrition Grade C+

Ingredients:

½ lb. skinless, boneless chicken breast

¾ cup vegetable broth

3 teaspoons lemon juice

3 teaspoons sesame oil

1 cup chopped spinach

2 tablespoons toasted almonds

¼ teaspoon pepper

Directions:

- Place the chicken in a saucepan then pour vegetable broth over the chicken and splash lemon juice over the chicken.

- Place the pan over medium heat then bring to boil. Once it is boiled, reduce the heat and bring to a simmer for approximately 15 minutes until the chicken is cooked.
- Take the chicken out from the pan and place it on a dish. Let it cool for a few minutes. Once the chicken is cool enough, cut the chicken into strips. Set aside.
- Pour sesame oil into a bowl then add 2 tablespoons of the liquid from the pan. Stir well.
- Arrange chopped spinach in a salad bowl then add chicken strips and almonds on top.
- Dust pepper on top then enjoy immediately.
- Garnish with pomegranate if you like.

Slow-Cooker BBQ Chicken

SmartPoints: 11

Serves: 4

Time: 6 hours, 45 minutes

Ingredients:

6 boneless, skinless chicken thighs

⅓ cup salted butter

¼ cup red wine vinegar

¼ cup Erythritol

¼ cup organic tomato paste

¼ cup chicken stock

2 tablespoons spicy brown mustard

2 tablespoons yellow mustard

1 tablespoon soy sauce

1 tablespoon liquid smoke

2 teaspoons chili powder

1 teaspoon cayenne pepper

1 teaspoon cumin

1 teaspoon Red Boat fish sauce

Directions:

1. Add the butter, chicken stock, vinegar, tomato paste, mustards, liquid smoke, soy sauce, fish sauce, and seasonings into a bowl.

2. Add the Erythritol sweetener and mix well.

3. Taste and adjust to your liking. More vinegar makes the sauce tangier, while more sweetener makes it sweeter.

4. Put the chicken thighs in the slow cooker and pour over the BBQ sauce.

5. Cook for 2 hours.

6. Open the lid and push down on the chicken, so it's beneath the juices.

7. Add the butter and swirl it around, so it gets on the chicken.

8. Cook for another 3-4 hours.

9. Shred the chicken.

10. With the lid on, keep cooking on high for another 45 minutes to reduce the sauce.

11. Mix one last time before serving!

Nutritional Info:

Total calories: 510

Carbs: 2.3

Fat: 30

Protein: 51.5

Fiber: 0

Weight Watchers Smart Points Cookbook

Roasted Chicken with Asparagus

SmartPoints: 6

Serving: 2

Nutrition Facts

Serving Size 381 g

Amount Per Serving

Calories 321

Calories from Fat 77

% Daily Value*

Total Fat 8.6g

13%

Saturated Fat 3.2g

16%

Trans Fat 0.0g

Cholesterol 132mg

44%

Sodium 179mg

7%

Potassium 298mg

9%

Total Carbohydrates 6.7g

2%

Dietary Fiber 3.0g

12%

Sugars 2.9g

Protein 54.0g

| Vitamin A 19% | • | Vitamin C 23% |
| Calcium 5% | • | Iron 26% |

Nutrition Grade B

* Based on a 2000 calorie diet

Ingredients:

- 1-½ teaspoons oregano
- 1 teaspoon minced garlic
- ¼ teaspoon black pepper
- 1 lb. skinless, boneless, chicken breast
- ½ lb. asparagus
- ¼ cup vegetable broth
- 3 teaspoons orange juice

Directions:

- Preheat an oven to 425 °F then lines a baking pan with aluminum foil. Set aside.

- Place oregano, minced garlic, and black pepper in a bowl then mix until well combined.
- Rub the chicken with the spice mixture until all sides are completely seasoned.
- Preheat a skillet then coat with cooking spray.
- Stir in the seasoned chicken then sauté until the chicken halved cooked.
- Pour vegetable broth into the skillet then cooked until the liquid is completely absorbed into the chicken.
- Once it is done, transfer the chicken into the prepared baking pan then bake for 15 minutes.
- Remove the chicken then place on a serving dish.
- After that, place the asparagus on the same baking pan, then bake for about 5 minutes, until the asparagus is tender and crispy.
- Serve the roasted chicken with asparagus.
- Enjoy!

Weight Watchers Smart Points Cookbook

Chicken Satay

SmartPoints: 4

Serving: 6

Nutrition Facts

Serving Size 92 g

Amount Per Serving

Calories 116

Calories from Fat 35

% Daily Value*

Total Fat 3.9g

6%

Saturated Fat 1.2g

6%

Trans Fat 0.0g

Cholesterol 44mg

15%

Sodium 329mg

14%

Potassium 43mg

Weight Watchers Smart Points Cookbook

1%

Total Carbohydrates 2.5g

1%

Sugars 1.3g

Protein 17.4g

| Vitamin A 2% | • | Vitamin C 3% |
| Calcium 1% | • | Iron 4% |

Nutrition Grade D+

* Based on a 2000 calorie diet

Ingredients:

- 1 lb. skinless, boneless, chicken breast
- 2 tablespoons soy sauce
- 2 tablespoons dry sherry
- 1-½ teaspoon sesame oil
- 1 teaspoon minced garlic
- 1 ½ teaspoon ginger powder
- 1 -teaspoon honey
- ½ cup chopped scallions

Directions:

- Combine soy sauce, dry sherry, sesame oil, minced garlic, honey, and ginger powder in a dish. Stir until well combined.

- Cut the chicken into cubes then place rub the chicken with soy sauce mixture.
- Marinate in the refrigerator for at least an hour then alternately prick marinated chicken and chopped scallions.
- Preheat a grill then grill the chicken satay. Don't forget to turn the satay occasionally so that the satay is cooked through.
- Serve and enjoy warm.

Easy Paprika Chicken

SmartPoints: 5

Serves: 4

Time: About 40 minutes

Ingredients:

4 boneless, skinless chicken breasts

3 tablespoons olive oil

2 tablespoons lemon juice

2 tablespoons Spanish smoked paprika

1 tablespoon low-carb maple syrup

2 teaspoons minced garlic

Salt and pepper to taste

Directions:

1. Preheat your oven to 350-degrees.

2. Cut the chicken into chunks and season with salt and pepper.

3. Mix the paprika, olive oil, garlic, and maple syrup together, making the sauce.

4. Spoon in ⅓ of the sauce into the bottom of a casserole dish and put the chicken on top.

5. Pour the rest of the sauce evenly on top of the chicken.

6. Bake for 30-35 minutes.

7. Broil for another 4-5 minutes before serving.

Nutritional Info:

Total calories: 274

Carbs: 2

Fat: 13.6

Protein: 36.4

Fiber: 1.5

Weight Watchers Smart Points Cookbook

Weight Watchers Smart Points Cookbook

FISH RECIPES

Weight Watchers Smart Points Cookbook

Baked Crispy Salmon

SmartPoints: 4

Serving: 6

Nutrition Facts

Serving Size 110 g

Amount Per Serving

Calories 175

Calories from Fat 81

% Daily Value*

Total Fat 8.9g

14%

Saturated Fat 1.4g

7%

Trans Fat 0.0g

Cholesterol 33mg

11%

Sodium 155mg

6%

Potassium 329mg

Weight Watchers Smart Points Cookbook

9%

Total Carbohydrates 6.7g

2%

Sugars 0.6g

Protein 17.1g

* Based on a 2000 calorie diet

Nutrition Facts

Ingredients:

2 egg whites

4 tablespoons water

½ cup breadcrumbs

4 tablespoons flour

1 lb. salmon fillet

2 tablespoons margarine, melted

¼ teaspoon pepper

Directions:

- Preheat an oven to 350 °F then lines a baking sheet with parchment paper. Set aside.

- Cut the salmon into slices then set aside.
- Combine egg whites water, breadcrumbs, and pepper in a bowl. Stir until incorporated.
- Dip the salmon slices in the egg mixture then roll with flour. Return the coated salmon to the egg mixture and roll again in the flour.
- Arrange the coated salmon on the prepared baking pan the drizzle with melted margarine.
- Bake for approximately 40 minutes until the salmon is completely cooked and the flour is crispy.
- Transfer the baked crispy salmon on a serving platter then serve warm.

Weight Watchers Smart Points Cookbook

Walnut-Crusted Baked Salmon Fillets

SmartPoints: 10

Serves: 2

Time: 12 minutes

Ingredients:

2, 3-ounce salmon fillets

½ cup walnuts

2 tablespoons sugar-free maple syrup

1 tablespoon Dijon mustard

1 tablespoon olive oil

¼ teaspoon dill

Salt and pepper to taste

Directions:

1. Preheat your oven to 350 degrees.

2. Put the maple syrup, mustard, nuts, and seasonings into a food processor and run until it becomes a paste.

3. Heat the olive oil in a skillet until very hot.

4. Pat the salmon dry and lay it skin-side down to sear for 3 minutes.

5. As the fish sears, spread the walnut paste on the open face of the fillets.

6. After 3 minutes, move the pan to the oven and bake for 8 minutes.

7. Serve and enjoy!

Nutritional Info:

Total calories: 373

Carbs: 3

Fat: 23

Protein: 14

Fiber: 1

Weight Watchers Smart Points Cookbook

Roasted Tomato Salmon

SmartPoints: 9

Serving: 2

Nutrition Facts

Serving Size 412 g

Amount Per Serving

Calories 486

Calories from Fat 192

% Daily Value*

Total Fat 21.4g

33%

Saturated Fat 3.1g

15%

Trans Fat 0.0g

Cholesterol 150mg

50%

Sodium 446mg

19%

Potassium 1534mg

44%

Total Carbohydrates 8.0g

3%

Dietary Fiber 1.6g

6%

Sugars 1.3g

Protein 67.4g

| Vitamin A 21% | • | Vitamin C 17% |
| Calcium 18% | • | Iron 20% |

Nutrition Grade B

* Based on a 2000 calorie diet

Ingredients:

1 ½ lbs. fresh salmon

½ cup cherry tomatoes

4 tablespoons sliced shallot

1 tablespoon minced garlic

3 teaspoons oregano

1 ½ teaspoons olive oil

¼ teaspoon salt

¼ teaspoon black pepper

Directions:

- Preheat an oven to 400 °F and coat a baking dish with cooking. Set aside.
- Place cherry tomatoes, sliced shallots, minced garlic, olive oil, and oregano in a bowl.
- Season with salt and black pepper then stir until well combined.
- Place the salmon in the prepared baking pan then pour the cherry tomatoes mixture over the salmon.
- Bake for approximately 30 minutes until the salmon completely cooked and easy to flakes when it is pricked with a fork.
- Transfer the roasted salmon to a serving dish together with the vegetables and spices.
- Serve and enjoy warm.
- Add some more vegetables as you desired.

Lean and Healthy Baked Cod

SmartPoints: 3

Serving: 4

Nutrition Facts

Serving Size 106 g

Amount Per Serving

Calories 147

Calories from Fat 32

% Daily Value*

Total Fat 3.6g

5%

Saturated Fat 0.6g

3%

Cholesterol 49mg

16%

Sodium 169mg

7%

Potassium 232mg

7%

Total Carbohydrates 7.1g

2%

Sugars 1.1g

Protein 20.5g

Ingredients:

- 2 tablespoons mayonnaise
- ¾ lb. cod
- 2 tablespoons chopped onion
- 4 tablespoons breadcrumbs
- 1 teaspoon chopped parsley
- 1 teaspoon lemon juice
- 2 teaspoons olive oil

Directions:

- Preheat and oven to 350 °F and place a large aluminum foil on a baking dish. Set aside.
- Place the cod on the aluminum foil then brush it with mayonnaise.
- Preheat a skillet with olive oil and when the oil is hot, stir in the chopped onion and sauté until wilted.
- Add the remaining ingredients into the skillet then stir until well combined.
- Pour the sautéed ingredients over the cod then wrap the cod with aluminum foil.

- Bake for approximately 30 minutes until the cod is tender and cooked through.
- Remove the cod from the oven then carefully unwrap the aluminum foil.
- Transfer the cod to a serving dish and enjoy.

Weight Watchers Smart Points Cookbook

Salmon Salads with Asparagus

SmartPoints: 3

Serving: 2

Nutrition Facts

Serving Size 556 g

Amount Per Serving

Calories 643

Calories from Fat 257

% Daily Value*

Total Fat 28.5g

44%

Saturated Fat 4.1g

21%

Trans Fat 0.0g

Cholesterol 200mg

67%

Sodium 685mg

29%

Potassium 1895mg

54%

Total Carbohydrates 6.4g

2%

Dietary Fiber 2.0g

8%

Sugars 2.5g

Protein 91.3g

| Vitamin A 15% | • | Vitamin C 25% |
| Calcium 18% | • | Iron 21% |

Nutrition Grade B-

Serving Size 29 g

Ingredients:

2 lbs. salmon fillet

2 tablespoons chopped leeks

½ cup chopped asparagus

½ cup peas

½ cup vegetable broth

¼ teaspoon salt

¼ teaspoon pepper

Directions:

- Make sure that there aren't any bones in the salmon.
- Prepare a Dutch oven then coat with cooking spray.

- Sprinkle the chopped leek on the bottom of the Dutch oven then arrange salmon on it.
- Put chopped asparagus and peas in the Dutch oven then pour vegetable broth over the salmon.
- Season with pepper and salt then cook on medium heat until it is boiled.
- Once it is boiled, reduce the heat and cover the Dutch oven with the lid.
- Cook for about 3o0 minutes until the salmon is not pink and the vegetables are tender enough.
- Once it is done, open the lid and transfer the salmon, peas, and asparagus to a serving dish.
- Pour a little amount of the liquid in the Dutch Oven over the almond salads.
- Serve and enjoy.

Spicy Tuna Salad

SmartPoints: 10

Total Time: 10 minutes

Serves: 2 Servings

Ingredients:

- 2 cans tuna, drained
- 1/4 tsp red pepper flakes
- 1/4 tsp dill
- 1/4 tsp black pepper
- 1 cup carrot, shredded
- 4 celery stalks, chopped
- 1/8 cup sriracha sauce
- 1/8 cup mustard
- 1/2 cup plain yogurt

Directions:

1. Add all ingredients into large mixing bowl and mix well until combine.

2. Serve immediately and enjoy.

Nutritional Value (Amount per Serving):

- Calories 451
- Fat 18.1 g
- Carbohydrates 14.6 g
- Sugar 8.2 g
- Protein 54.0 g
- Cholesterol 59 mg

Salmon Poke Bowl

SmartPoints: 10

Serves: 2

Time: 25 minutes

Ingredients:

½ pound sushi-grade, skinless, boneless salmon

2 chopped medium-sized green onions

2 tablespoons coconut aminos

1 tablespoon fresh lemon juice

1 tablespoon sesame seeds

1 tablespoon toasted sesame oil

1 teaspoon rice vinegar

1 teaspoon Sriracha

2 cups cauliflower rice

1 tablespoon rice vinegar

1 tablespoon coconut oil

¼ teaspoon salt

Directions:

1. Mix the coconut aminos, lemon juice, vinegar, salt, and toasted sesame oil together.

2. Cut the salmon into ½-1 inch pieces.

3. Put the fish in a bowl and pour in the marinade, along with the sesame seeds and green onions.

4. Add the sriracha and mix well.

5. Store in the fridge while you make the cauliflower rice.

6. Run the cauliflower through a food processor to get a grain-like texture that fills 2 cups.

7. Grease a pan with butter and heat.

8. When hot, put in the cauliflower rice and cook for 5-7 minutes, stirring so the rice doesn't stick and burn.

9. In a small bowl, mix salt and vinegar.

10. When the cauliflower is done, remove from heat and mix with the vinegar.

11. Serve the raw salmon on top, with your choice of toppings, including avocado slices, cucumber, daikon, and/or pickled ginger.

Nutritional Info:

Total calories: 400

Carbs: 8.5

Fat: 42.4

Protein: 30.3

Fiber: 8.8

Salmon with Mushroom and Spinach

SmartPoints: 12

Total Time: 35 minutes

Serves: 2 Servings

Ingredients:

- 1 lb salmon fillets, with skin
- 1 tbsp lemon juice
- 3 tbsp olive oil
- 1/2 tsp garlic powder
- 1 cup tomato, chopped
- 2 cups fresh spinach, chopped
- 2 medium mushrooms, sliced
- Parmesan cheese, grated
- Black pepper

- Salt

Directions:

1. Preheat the oven at 375 F.
2. Wash salmon fillet and dry with paper towel.
3. Season with pepper and salt.
4. Spray baking dish with cooking spray and place salmon fillet skin side down in dish.
5. Combine remaining ingredients except parmesan cheese and spoon over the fish fillet.
6. Bake in preheated oven for 25 minutes.
7. Sprinkle grated parmesan cheese and serve.

Nutritional Value (Amount per Serving):

- Calories 511
- Fat 35.4 g
- Carbohydrates 5.9 g
- Sugar 3.1 g
- Protein 46.4 g
- Cholesterol 100 mg

Cucumber Sushi Rolls

SmartPoints: 7

Serves: 2

Time: 30 minutes

Ingredients:

2 cucumbers

½ pound tuna steak

½ avocado

2 tablespoons mayo

1 green onion stalk

2 teaspoons Sriracha

½ teaspoon sesame seeds

Directions:

1. Peel the cucumber and cut off the ends.

2. Choose a long, sharp knife, and run it under water, so it's wet.

3. Carefully cut along the outside of the cucumber; you should be able to just see the knife through the transparent fruit, so about 1/10 of an inch. You are basically cutting a "sheet" of cucumber, which you will roll.

4. When you've reached the seeds, you're done cutting.

5. Slice the raw tuna into thin squares, and the avocado into slices.

6. Mix the mayo and hot sauce together.

7. Spread out your cucumber roll and lay down the fish on one side. Top the fish with some avocado slices.

8. Roll tightly, beginning on the end with the fish.

9. When you've almost finished the roll, spread the spicy mayo on the cucumber and complete the roll, so the mayo sticks the roll together.

10. Cut the cucumber into ½-1 inch rounds.

11. Repeat with the second cucumber, so you get about 12 sushi pieces in total, which is enough for two people.

12. Garnish with chopped green onion and sesame seeds!

Nutritional Info:

Total calories: 322

Carbs: 2.5

Fat: 17

Protein: 36

Fiber: 3.9

Simple Lemon Wild Salmon

SmartPoints: 4

Total Time: 25 minutes

Serves: 4 Servings

Ingredients:

- 1 lb wild salmon
- 1/2 tsp parsley
- 1/2 tsp tarragon
- 2 tbsp lemon juice
- 1/2 tsp dill weeds
- 3 garlic cloves, minced
- 1 tbsp olive oil

Directions:

1. Preheat the oven at 300 F.
2. Add olive oil, minced garlic, lemon juice and herbs in bowl and mix well.

3. Spray baking sheet with cooking spray then place salmon on baking sheet and spared herbs mixture over the salmon.

4. Bake salmon about 20 minutes.

5. Serve salmon with steam rice and enjoy.

Nutritional Value (Amount per Serving):

- Calories 186
- Fat 10.6 g
- Carbohydrates 1.0 g
- Sugar 0.2 g
- Protein 22.2 g
- Cholesterol 50 mg

BEEF RECIPES

Weight Watchers Smart Points Cookbook

Beef Steak in Tomato Sauce

SmartPoints: 4

Serving: 2

Nutrition Facts

Serving Size 354 g

Amount Per Serving

Calories 135

Calories from Fat 77

% Daily Value*

Total Fat 8.6g

13%

Saturated Fat 1.4g

7%

Cholesterol 0mg

0%

Sodium 770mg

32%

Weight Watchers Smart Points Cookbook

Potassium 473mg

14%

Total Carbohydrates 9.3g

3%

Dietary Fiber 1.3g

5%

Sugars 3.1g

Protein 6.1g

* Based on a 2000 calorie diet

Nutrition Facts

Ingredients:

- 1 lb. Beef without fat
- 3 teaspoons olive oil
- 2 tablespoons minced shallots
- 1 teaspoon minced garlic
- 1 cup diced tomato
- 2 cups vegetable broth
- 2 teaspoons cornstarch
- 1 tablespoon chopped parsley

¼ teaspoon black pepper

Directions:

- Preheat an oven to 350 °F then pours olive oil into a baking pan.
- Place the beef into the prepared baking pan and bake for about 3 minutes then flip the beef.
- Continue to bake for another 3 minutes then remove the beef from the oven.
- Place the baked beef on a serving dish then cover with aluminum foil to keep it warm.
- Pour the remaining liquid from the baking pan into a skillet.
- Add minced shallots, minced garlic, and tomato into the skillet then pour vegetable broth over the ingredients.
- Bring to boil and stir until the tomato is completely dissolved.
- Combine the cornstarch with a little amount of water then pour the mixture into the sauce. Bring to a simmer until the sauce is thickened.
- Unwrap the cooked beef then pour the sauce over the beef.
- Sprinkle black pepper on top and garnish with chopped parsley.
- Serve and enjoy warm.

Weight Watchers Smart Points Cookbook

Beef Patty Cucumber Salad

SmartPoints: 14

Serving: 4

Nutrition Facts

Serving Size 552 g

Weight Watchers Smart Points Cookbook

Amount Per Serving

Calories 505

Total Fat 40.7g

Sodium 71mg

3%

Total Carbohydrates 20.4g

7%

Sugars 8.4g

Protein 4.5g

Vitamin A 7%	•	Vitamin C 24%
Calcium 19%	•	Iron 19%

Nutrition Grade D

Ingredients:

PATTIES

- ¼ cup chopped onion
- 1 teaspoon olive oil
- 1 cup minced beef
- ¼ cup grated beetroot
- 1 teaspoon diced garlic
- 1 tablespoon chopped rosemary
- 1 teaspoon black pepper powder
- 1 cup olive oil, for frying
- 1 cup sliced cucumber

CUCUMBER SALADS

- 1 cup sliced cucumber
- 1 teaspoon lemon zest
- 3 teaspoons sesame seeds
- 2 tablespoons apple cider vinegar
- ½ teaspoon Dijon mustard
- ¼ teaspoon black pepper powder

GARNISH

- Fresh lettuce
- Fresh parsley

Instructions:

1. Preheat a skillet then pour olive oil into the skillet.
2. Once it is hot, stir in onion and sauté until wilted and aromatic.
3. Place the sautéed onion together with the patties ingredients in a bowl and mix well.
4. Using your hands, mold the mixture into small patties.
5. Preheat a frying pan then pour a cup of olive oil into the pan.
6. Once it is hot, arrange the patties on the pan and cook for approximately 6 minutes.

7. Carefully flip the patties and cook another side for 6 minutes as well—the beetroot can easily burn so avoid high heat in frying the patties.
8. Once the patties are cooked, remove from the pan and let them cool for a few minutes.
9. Meanwhile, combine the salad ingredients in a bowl and mix until incorporated.
10. Arrange fresh lettuce on a serving dish then put the patties on the lettuce.
11. Drizzle sauce over the patties and garnish with fresh parsley.
12. Serve and enjoy at dinner.

Weight Watchers Smart Points Cookbook

Brown Beef Potato Stew

SmartPoints: 4

Serving: 5

Nutrition Facts

Serving Size 183 g

Amount Per Serving

Calories 138

Calories from Fat 7

% Daily Value*

Total Fat 4.8g

1%

Cholesterol 0mg

0%

Sodium 1286mg

54%

Potassium 251mg

7%

Total Carbohydrates 3.9g

1%

Dietary Fiber 0.7g

3%

Sugars 1.8g

Protein 7.9g

| Vitamin A 8% | • | Vitamin C 11% |
| Calcium 1% | • | Iron 4% |

Nutrition Grade A

*Based on a 2000 calorie diet

Ingredients:

1 lb. beef

½ cup potato cubes

1 teaspoon minced garlic

4 cup beef broth

2 tablespoons soy sauce

¼ teaspoon pepper

1 teaspoon olive oil

Directions:

- Cut the beef into cubes then set aside.
- Preheat a stockpot over medium heat the put olive oil in it.
- Stir in garlic and sauté until wilted and aromatic.
- Add the beef together with potato cubes then stirring occasionally.

- Pour the beef stock over the beef and potatoes then add soy sauce and season with pepper. Stir until well combined.
- Bring to a simmer for approximately 30 minutes until the beef is tender and cooked completely.
- Transfer the beef stew to a serving bowl then enjoy hot.

Spiced Beef Stew with Carrots and Blueberries

SmartPoints: 6

Serving: 3

Nutrition Facts

Serving Size 96 g

Amount Per Serving

Calories 152

Calories from Fat 112

% Daily Value*

Total Fat 12.4g

19%

Saturated Fat 1.6g

8%

Trans Fat 0.0g

Cholesterol 0mg

0%

Sodium 182mg

Weight Watchers Smart Points Cookbook

8%

Potassium 209mg

6%

Total Carbohydrates 10.1g

3%

Dietary Fiber 2.2g

9%

Sugars 5.1g

Protein 1.9g

| Vitamin A 123% | • | Vitamin C 12% |
| Calcium 3% | • | Iron 4% |

Nutrition Grade B+

* Based on a 2000 calorie diet

Ingredients:
- 2 cups chopped beef
- ½ cup fresh blueberries
- 1 cup chopped carrots
- 1 tablespoon almond butter
- 2 tablespoons olive oil
- ¼ teaspoon sea salt
- ¼ teaspoon black pepper
- ¼ teaspoon garlic powder
- ½ cup sliced onion

Instructions:
1. Preheat a skillet then pour olive oil into the skillet.
2. Once it is hot, stir in chopped beef and onion then sauté until the onion is aromatic and the beef is wilted.
3. Season the beef with sea salt, black pepper powder, and garlic powder.
4. Add the chopped carrots and cook stir until cooked.
5. Last, add in the blueberries and butter then stir until the butter melts.
6. Transfer the cooked beef to a serving dish and serve warm.

Korean Beef-Stuffed Peppers

SmartPoints: 12

Serves: 4

Time: 20-25 minutes

Stuffed bell peppers are a great alternative to hamburgers, especially when you fill the veggie with Korean barbeque. The beef is complimented with delicious ingredients like garlic, ginger, chili paste, and sugar-free apricot preserves for a spicy-sweet flavor.

Ingredients:

1 pound ground beef

8 big eggs

2 halved bell peppers

2 thinly-sliced spring onions

2 teaspoons minced ginger

2 teaspoons minced garlic

Salt and pepper to taste

⅓ cup sugar-free apricot preserves

1 ½ tablespoons rice wine vinegar

1 tablespoon chili paste

1 tablespoon soy sauce

1 tablespoons reduced-sugar ketchup

Directions:

1. Brown the beef on medium-high heat.

2. As it browns, season with salt, pepper, garlic, and ginger, and mix.

3. When meat is browned, push it aside, and add the sliced onions.

4. Let them fry for 1-2 minutes before removing the pan from the heat.

5. In another pan, mix all the ingredients in the second list and reduce, so it thickens.

6. Mix ½ of the sauce into the beef pan.

7. Stuff the pepper halves with the beef and cook at 350-degrees for 12-15 minutes.

8. While the peppers bake, fry the eggs.

9. When time is up, take out the peppers and brush the rest of the sauce on top.

10. Serve the peppers with two fried eggs per half.

Nutritional Info:

Total calories: 470

Carbs: 6.3

Fat: 35

Protein: 32.2

Fiber: 5.3

Weight Watchers Smart Points Cookbook

Spicy Beef and Butternut Squash Stew

SmartPoints: 7

Serving: 1

Nutrition Facts

Serving Size 606 g

Amount Per Serving

Calories 182

Calories from Fat 129

% Daily Value*

Total Fat 14.4g

22%

Saturated Fat 2.1g

11%

Trans Fat 0.0g

Cholesterol 0mg

0%

Sodium 93mg

4%

Potassium 437mg

12%

Total Carbohydrates 14.5g

5%

Dietary Fiber 4.2g

17%

Sugars 6.5g

Protein 1.5g

Vitamin A 387%   •   Vitamin C 15%

Calcium 8%   •   Iron 6%

Nutrition Grade B+

* Based on a 2000 calorie diet

Ingredients:
- 1 tablespoon olive oil
- 2 cups cubed beef
- 1 teaspoon minced garlic
- 2 teaspoons minced sage
- ¼ teaspoon smoked paprika
- 1 tablespoon chopped red chilies
- 2 cups cubed butternut squash
- 1 cup chopped carrots
- 2 cups water

- ¼ teaspoon pepper powder

Instructions:
1. Preheat olive oil in a Dutch oven over medium heat. Once it is hot, brown the cubed beef until half cooked and wilted. Set aside.
2. Toss the minced garlic, sage, chopped red chilies and smoked paprika in the skillet then season with pepper powder.
3. Return the cooked beef into the skillet together with cubed butternut squash and carrots then pour water over the beef.
4. Bring to boil then reduce the heat and cook for an hour or more until the beef is tender.
5. Transfer the stew to a serving bowl then enjoy hot.

Weight Watchers Smart Points Cookbook

Sautéed Beef Onion

SmartPoints: 9

Serving: 2

Nutrition Facts

Serving Size 286 g

Amount Per Serving

Calories 447

Calories from Fat 128

% Daily Value*

Total Fat 14.2g

22%

Saturated Fat 5.3g

27%

Cholesterol 203mg

68%

Sodium 443mg

18%

Potassium 1011mg

29%

Total Carbohydrates 6.0g

2%

Dietary Fiber 1.5g

6%

Sugars 2.4g

Protein 69.5g

| Vitamin A 0% | • | Vitamin C 7% |
| Calcium 2% | • | Iron 239% |

Nutrition Grade B+

* Based on a 2000 calorie diet

Ingredients:

- 1 lb. beef without fat
- 1 cup chopped onion
- 1 teaspoon ground black pepper
- ¼ teaspoon salt
- 2 tablespoons olive oil
- 1 cup water

Directions:

- Cut the beef into medium cubes then set aside.

- Preheat a skillet over medium heat and pour olive oil into the skillet.
- Once it is hot, stir in chopped onion and sauté until wilted and aromatic.
- Add the beef into the skillet then pour water into the skillet.
- Season with salt then bring to boil.
- Once it is boiled, reduce the heat and continue to cook until the beef is tender.
- Transfer the cooked beef to a serving dish then sprinkle ground black pepper over the beef.
- Serve and enjoy.

Weight Watchers Smart Points Cookbook

PORK RECIPES

Weight Watchers Smart Points Cookbook

Delicious Pork with Sour Strawberry Sauce

SmartPoints: 5

Serving: 2

Nutrition Facts

Serving Size 240 g

Amount Per Serving

Calories 237

Calories from Fat 72

% Daily Value*

Total Fat 8.0g

12%

Saturated Fat 1.7g

9%

Trans Fat 0.1g

Cholesterol 83mg

28%

Sodium 708mg

Weight Watchers Smart Points Cookbook

30%

Potassium 640mg

18%

Total Carbohydrates 8.0g

3%

Dietary Fiber 1.2g

5%

Sugars 2.8g

Protein 32.1g

Vitamin A 0%   •   Vitamin C 38%

Calcium 2%   •   Iron 11%

Nutrition Grade A-

* Based on a 2000 calorie diet

Ingredients:

½ cup vegetable broth

½ cup chopped strawberries

1 tablespoon Stevia

1-tablespoon soy sauce

1 teaspoon minced garlic

½ lb. pork tenderloin

1-teaspoon garlic powder

¼ teaspoon pepper

1 -½ teaspoons canola oil

1 ½ teaspoons cornstarch

1 ½ teaspoons cold water

2 tablespoons chopped onion

Directions:

- Place chopped strawberries, Stevia, soy sauce, and minced garlic in a saucepan.
- Pour vegetable broth into the saucepan then bring to boil.
- Once it is boiled, reduce the heat then bring to a simmer until the sauce is thickened.
- Strain the sauce and discard the solids. Set aside.
- Next, season the pork tenderloin with garlic powder and pepper. Rub thoroughly until the pork is completely seasoned.
- Preheat a skillet over medium heat then pour canola oil into the skillet.
- Once it is hot, stir in the pork and cook until brown. Remove the cooked pork from the skillet and place on a plate.
- Pour the strawberry sauce into the skillet then pour cornstarch and water mixture into the skillet.
- Keep stirring until the sauce is thickened then return the pork into the skillet.
- Stir until the pork is completely coated with sauce then transfer the pork to a serving dish together with the sauce.
- Top with onion and garnish with fresh strawberries if you desired.
- Enjoy warm.

Weight Watchers Smart Points Cookbook

Tasty Pork Meatballs in Tomato Sauce

SmartPoints: 6

Serving: 6

Nutrition Facts

Serving Size 328 g

Amount Per Serving

Calories 351

Calories from Fat 7

% Daily Value*

Total Fat 8g

Trans Fat 0.0g

Sodium 6mg

0%

Potassium 29mg

1%

Total Carbohydrates 5.2g

Weight Watchers Smart Points Cookbook

0%

Sugars 0.5g

Protein 0.8g

| Vitamin A 0% | • | Vitamin C 1% |
| Calcium 0% | • | Iron 0% |

Nutrition Grade B+

* Based on a 2000 calorie diet

Ingredients:
- 1 ½ cups chopped pork
- 1 organic egg white
- ½ cup chopped onion
- 3 teaspoons coconut flour
- 1 teaspoon olive oil
- ¾ teaspoon ginger powder
- 1 cup mashed tomato
- 4 tablespoons water
- 2 teaspoons apple cider vinegar
- ¼ teaspoon garlic powder

Instructions:

1. First, make the sauce by combining mashed tomato, water, apple cider vinegar, garlic powder, and ¼ teaspoon ginger powder in a pot then bring to a simmer. Set aside.

2. Next, preheat an oven to 350 °F and line a baking pan with parchment paper. Set aside.
3. Meanwhile, place the chopped pork, egg white, onion, coconut flour, olive oil, and ginger powder together with ginger powder in a food processor.
4. Process until well combined and shape into small meatballs.
5. Arrange the meatballs on the prepared baking pan and bake for approximately 12 minutes.
6. Transfer the baked meatballs to a serving dish then pour sauce over the meatballs.

Serve and enjoy immediately.

Sunflower-Butter Pork Kabobs

SmartPoints: 4

Serves: 4

Time: 1 hour, 15 minutes

Sunflower butter is made from sunflower seeds, and has that same nutty-sweet, summery flavor. It's less intense than peanut butter, so the other flavors in the pork like the hot sauce, garlic, and crushed red pepper really come through.

Ingredients:

1 pound pork

1 medium-sized green bell pepper

3 tablespoons sunflower butter

1 tablespoon minced garlic

1 tablespoon soy sauce

1 tablespoon water

2 teaspoons hot sauce (like Sriracha)

½ teaspoon crushed red pepper

Directions:

1. Mix everything but the pork in a food processor until smooth.

2. Cut the pork into bite-sized pieces and mix in a bowl with the marinade.

3. Let the pork marinate for at least 1 hour.

4. Chop the green pepper into skewer-ready pieces.

5. Skewer the meat and pepper alternately on metal skewers.

6. Broil for five minutes per side on high until the meat is 145-degrees.

7. Serve and enjoy!

Nutritional Info (1 kabob):

Total calories: 200

Carbs: 5

Fat: 8

Protein: 24

Fiber: 2

Weight Watchers Smart Points Cookbook

Delicious Pork in Blanket

SmartPoints: 6

Serving: 1

Ingredients:
- 1 lb. pork meat without fat
- 2 cups homemade barbecue sauce
- 12 slices bacon
- Fresh chopped lettuce, chopped cabbage, and lemon slices for garnish

Instructions:
1. Cut the pork into 6 medium cubes then place in a bowl with a lid.
2. Pour barbecue sauce over the cubed pork and marinate for at least 8 hours or overnight.
3. Place two slices of bacon on a flat surface then put a cube of pork on the top of the bacon.
4. Carefully wrap the pork with bacon then secure with a toothpicks.
5. Repeat with the remaining ingredients.
6. Preheat a grill over medium heat.
7. Once it is hot, grill the wrapped pork then flips until the pork is no longer pink and completely cooked.
8. Arrange the grilled pork on a serving dish and serve with fresh cabbage, lettuce, and lemon slice.
9. Enjoy right away.

Total calories: 220

Carbs: 5

Fat: 10

Protein: 32

… *Weight Watchers Smart Points Cookbook*

Pork Chops w/ a Cumin Crust

SmartPoints: 9

Serves: 3

Time: Around 25-30 minutes

Ingredients:

1 ½ pounds of pork chops

¼ cup golden flaxseed

2 stalks celery

1 orange pepper

½ white onion

¼ cup white wine

3 tablespoons coconut oil

2 teaspoons cumin

1 teaspoon cardamom

1 teaspoon coriander

Salt and pepper to taste

Directions:

1. Season the meat with salt and pepper.

2. Mix the flaxseed and spices together. These will form the crust.

3. Lay the chops in the crust mixture on both sides till well-coated.

4. Pour 3 tablespoons of coconut oil into a skillet and heat.

5. When the oil starts to smoke, put the pork chops in the skillet.

6. After 7 minutes, flip over, and cook for another 7 minutes on medium-low.

7. When the pork reaches 145-degrees, it's cooked through.

8. Wrap the chops in foil and rest on a pan.

9. Add the veggies to the pan with the meat juices.

10. Pour in the white wine and cook the veggies until they're soft.

11. Serve the pork chops with veggies.

Nutritional Info:

Total calories: 439

Carbs: 4.3

Fat: 23.7

Protein: 50.3

Fiber: 4.6

Weight Watchers Smart Points Cookbook

Spicy Pork Ribs

SmartPoints: 12

Serving: 4

Nutrition Facts

Serving Size 448 g

Amount Per Serving

Calories 401

% Daily Value*

Total Fat 30.7g

Saturated Fat 10.6g

Cholesterol 0mg

0%

Sodium 29mg

1%

Potassium 185mg

5%

Total Carbohydrates 7.7g

3%

Dietary Fiber 3.1g

12%

Sugars 1.7g

Protein 1.4g

Vitamin A 40% • Vitamin C 13%

Calcium 5% • Iron 9%

Nutrition Grade D+

Ingredients:
- 2 lb. pork rib without fat
- ½ tablespoon minced garlic
- ¼ cup chopped onion
- 1 teaspoon paprika
- 1 teaspoon coriander
- 1 teaspoon oregano
- 1 teaspoon red chili powder
- ½ cup olive oil
- ½ teaspoon cinnamon powder
- Lemon slices, for garnish

Instructions:

1. Combine minced garlic, chopped onion, paprika, coriander, oregano, and red chili powder in a bowl. Stir until incorporated.
2. Rub the pork rib with the mixture and marinate for approximately 30 minutes.
3. Preheat an oven to 300 °F and prepare a baking pan.
4. Wrap the marinated pork rib with aluminum foil then place on the baking pan and bake for 60 minutes.
5. Meanwhile, combine the olive oil with cinnamon powder, set aside.
6. Remove the cooked pork rib from the oven and discard the aluminum foil.
7. Grease the cooked pork with applesauce mixture then return into the oven and bake for another 30 minutes.
8. Once it is done, remove from the oven then transfer to a serving dish.
9. Garnish with lemon slices then serve hot.

# DESSERT RECIPES

Weight Watchers Smart Points Cookbook

Refreshing Mango Ice Cream

SmartPoints: 8

Serving: 2

Nutrition Facts
Serving Size 85 g

Amount Per Serving
Calories 207
Calories from Fat 151
% Daily Value*
Total Fat 16.8g
26%
Saturated Fat 12.2g
61%
Cholesterol 33mg
11%
Sodium 15mg
1%
Potassium 249mg
7%
Total Carbohydrates 15.1g
5%
Dietary Fiber 1.9g
8%
Sugars 12.5g
Protein 2.0g

Vitamin A 14% • Vitamin C 26%
Calcium 3% • Iron 3%
Nutrition Grade C+
* Based on a 2000 calorie diet
Nutrition Facts

Ingredients:

½ cup coconut milk

1 cup chopped mango

1 cup whipped cream

Directions:

Place the chopped mango in a blender then blend until smooth. Set aside.

Keep whipped cream, coconut milk, and the whisker in freezer for about 10 minutes until cold—this will make the whipped cream gets whipped into maximum volume in minimum time.

Remove from the freezer then place in a mixing bowl.

Whisk the whipped cream and coconut milk until smooth and fluffy.

After that, add the mango puree into the whipped cream mixture and whisk until incorporated.

Pour the ice cream mixture into a container and spread evenly. Cover with plastic wrap then freeze for about 4 hours until the ice cream becomes half frozen.

Remove the ice cream from the container then cut into medium pieces.

Place the ice cream pieces in a blender then blend until smooth.

Return the ice cream mixture into the container and re-wrap it again.

Freeze the ice cream until completely sets.

Once it is done, scoop the ice cream and put in a serving cup.

Serve and enjoy immediately.

Weight Watchers Smart Points Cookbook

Creamy Cherry Sorbet

SmartPoints: 5

Serving: 2

Nutrition Facts
Serving Size 214 g

Amount Per Serving
Calories 146
Calories from Fat 26
% Daily Value*
Total Fat 2.9g
4%
Saturated Fat 2.2g
11%
Cholesterol 14mg
5%
Sodium 143mg
6%
Potassium 448mg
13%
Total Carbohydrates 14.4g
5%
Sugars 14.3g
Protein 11.5g

| Vitamin A 2% | • | Vitamin C 2% |
| Calcium 37% | • | Iron 1% |

Nutrition Grade A
* Based on a 2000 calorie diet
Nutrition Facts
Serving Size 214 g

Ingredients:

¾ cup plain yogurt

1-cup cherries

2 tablespoons milk

Directions:

Combine cherries and yogurt in a blender then blend until smooth.

Add milk into the blender and re-blend for about 30 seconds until incorporated.

Pour the mixture into serving bowls then garnish with fresh cherries if you like.

Enjoy immediately.

Oat Banana Cookies

SmartPoints: 10

Serving: 4

Nutrition Facts
Serving Size 111 g

Amount Per Serving
Calories 327
Calories from Fat 149
% Daily Value*
Total Fat 16.5g
25%
Saturated Fat 3.2g
16%
Trans Fat 0.0g
Cholesterol 0mg
0%
Sodium 3mg
0%
Potassium 352mg
10%
Total Carbohydrates 41.0g
14%
Dietary Fiber 5.9g
24%
Sugars 7.3g
Protein 6.0g

Vitamin A 1%   •   Vitamin C 8%
Calcium 3%   •   Iron 11%
Nutrition Grade B+
* Based on a 2000 calorie diet

Ingredients:

1 ½ cup chopped banana

2 cups oats

¼ cup vegetable oil

1-teaspoon cinnamon

Directions:

Preheat an oven to 350 °F then lines a baking sheet with parchment paper.

Using a potato masher, mash the banana until smooth then add oats and the remaining ingredients into the mashed banana.

Using a wooden spatula, mix all of the ingredients until well combined.

Scoop the mixture then drop on the prepared baking sheet.

Do the same with the remaining mixture and arrange on the baking sheet.

Bake for approximately 20 minutes until the cookies are lightly brown.

Remove from the oven and transfer to a cooling rack.

Place the cookies in a jar then serve.

Weight Watchers Smart Points Cookbook

Almond Mango Mint Popsicles

SmartPoints: 5

Serving: 8

Nutrition Facts
Serving Size 55 g

Amount Per Serving
Calories 107
Calories from Fat 52
% Daily Value*
Total Fat 5.8g
9%
Saturated Fat 4.9g
25%
Cholesterol 0mg
0%
Sodium 9mg
0%
Potassium 218mg
6%
Total Carbohydrates 14.3g
5%
Dietary Fiber 1.8g
7%
Sugars 12.8g
Protein 1.7g

Vitamin A 8% • Vitamin C 25%
Calcium 2% • Iron 3%
Nutrition Grade B+
* Based on a 2000 calorie diet

Nutrition Facts

Ingredients:

2 ripe mangoes

¾ cup almond milk

¼ cup plain yogurt

4 mint leaves

Directions:

Peel the mangoes then cut into cubes.
Place the mango cubes in a blender then pour almond milk and plain yogurt into the blender.
Blend until smooth and incorporated.
Pour the mixture into 4 Popsicle molds then put a mint leaf into each popsicles.
Put a stick in each Popsicle then keep in the freezer for at least 3 hours.
Serve and enjoy.

Weight Watchers Smart Points Cookbook

Orange Peach Popsicles

SmartPoints: 1

Serving: 8

Nutrition Facts
Serving Size 29 g

Amount Per Serving
Calories 14
Calories from Fat 1
% Daily Value*
Total Fat 0.1g
0%
Cholesterol 0mg
0%
Sodium 1mg
0%
Potassium 63mg
2%
Total Carbohydrates 3.0g
1%
Sugars 2.7g
Protein 0.3g

Vitamin A 1%	•	Vitamin C 20%
Calcium 0%	•	Iron 1%

Nutrition Grade A-
* Based on a 2000 calorie diet

Nutrition Facts
Serving Size 29 g

Ingredients:

1 lb. peaches

2 tablespoons lemon juice

¼ cup orange juice

½ teaspoon vanilla extract

¼ cup strawberry chunks

Directions:

Peel the peaches then discard the seeds.

Chop the peeled peaches then place in a food processor together with vanilla extract.

Pour orange juice and splash lemon juice over the peaches then blend until become puree.

Transfer the mixture to a bowl then add strawberry chunks in it. Stir until just combined.

Divide the mixture into 8 Popsicle mold then freeze for approximately an hour.

After an hour, put a stick into each Popsicle then re-freeze again for at least 3 hours.

Remove from the freezer then enjoy.

Mango Silk Pudding

SmartPoints: 6

Serving: 6

Nutrition Facts
Serving Size 59 g

Amount Per Serving
Calories 145
Calories from Fat 63
% Daily Value*
Total Fat 7.0g
11%
Saturated Fat 5.5g
27%
Cholesterol 7mg
2%
Sodium 24mg
1%
Potassium 199mg
6%
Total Carbohydrates 13.8g
5%
Dietary Fiber 1.7g
7%
Sugars 12.2g
Protein 9.2g

Vitamin A 9% • Vitamin C 25%
Calcium 2% • Iron 3%
Nutrition Grade B-
* Based on a 2000 calorie diet

Nutrition Facts

Ingredients:

2 cups mango cubes

2 packages gelatin sheets

½ cup coconut milk

¼ cup heavy cream

Directions:

Place the gelatin sheets in a dish then pour cold water in it. Soak for a few minutes until soft.

Place the soft gelatin in a pot together with half of the coconut milk over very low heat. Stir until the gelatin is completely dissolved. Let it cool.

Place the mango cubes in a blender then pour the remaining coconut milk. Blend until smooth and creamy.

Combine the creamy mango, gelatin mixture, and heavy cream in a bowl then stir well.

Strain the mixture and pour into serving cups.

Chill the pudding in the refrigerator for at least 3 hours until set.

Once you want to consume, remove from the refrigerator then enjoy.

Weight Watchers Smart Points Cookbook

No Crust Pumpkin Cheesecake

SmartPoints: 10

Serving: 8

Nutrition Facts
Serving Size 98 g

Amount Per Serving
Calories 220
Calories from Fat 183
% Daily Value*
Total Fat 20.3g
31%
Saturated Fat 12.1g
61%
Trans Fat 0.0g
Cholesterol 152mg
51%
Sodium 151mg
6%
Potassium 142mg
4%
Total Carbohydrates 4.3g
1%
Dietary Fiber 1.0g
4%
Sugars 1.3g
Protein 5.8g

| Vitamin A 112% | • | Vitamin C 2% |
| Calcium 6% | • | Iron 7% |

Nutrition Grade D+

Ingredients:

1 ½ cups cream cheese

1-teaspoon vanilla extract

½ teaspoon cinnamon

¼ teaspoon nutmeg

2 fresh eggs

2 egg yolks

1 cup pumpkin puree

4 tablespoons heavy cream

Directions:

Preheat an oven to 350 °F and prepare a 7-inch spring form pan.

Place cream cheese, cinnamon, vanilla, and nutmeg in a mixing bowl.

Using an electric mixer beat the cream cheese until fluffy then adds eggs into the bowl.

Continue to beat then add pumpkin puree and heavy cream. Mix until smooth and incorporated.

Pour the mixture into the prepared spring form pan then spread evenly.

Bake for about an hour until it sets then remove from the oven and let it cool for 15 minutes.

Once the cheesecake is cool, run a knife inside the pan to release the cake.

Place the cake on a serving dish then refrigerate for at least 4 hours before serving.

Enjoy!

Weight Watchers Smart Points Cookbook

Fruit Pastry Tart

SmartPoints: 10

Serving: 8

Nutrition Facts
Serving Size 111 g

Amount Per Serving
Calories 215
Calories from Fat 162
% Daily Value*
Total Fat 18.0g
28%
Saturated Fat 10.7g
54%
Cholesterol 109mg
36%
Sodium 111mg
5%
Potassium 125mg
4%
Total Carbohydrates 10.7g
4%
Dietary Fiber 0.8g
3%
Sugars 3.7g
Protein 3.7g

Vitamin A 13%   Vitamin C 17%
Calcium 3%   Iron 4%
Nutrition Grade C+
* Based on a 2000 calorie diet
Nutrition Facts

Ingredients:

1-cup water

½ cup butter

½ cup multi-purpose flour

3 eggs

TOPPING:

1 cup whipped cream

1 kiwi

1 peach

1/2 cup red grapes

Directions:

Preheat an oven to 350 °F then greases a baking sheet with butter or cooking spray then set aside.
Place water and butter in a saucepan over low heat.
Once the butter is melted, add the flour then stir vigorously until incorporated.
Remove from the heat and let it cool.
Once the batter is cool, add eggs into the batter and mix until well combined.
Pipe the batter on the prepared baking sheet then bake for about 12 minutes—do not open the oven until the choux is completely cooked.
Remove from the oven and let them cool.
Cut the top of the choux then arrange on a serving dish.
Pipe whipped cream on the choux then arrange sliced kiwi, sliced peach, and grapes on the top.
Garnish with any kind of ingredients, as you desired.
Serve and enjoy.

Weight Watchers Smart Points Cookbook

Apricot Rice Pudding

SmartPoints: 3

Serving: 4

Nutrition Facts
Serving Size 53 g

Amount Per Serving
Calories 86
Calories from Fat 33
% Daily Value*
Total Fat 3.6g
6%
Saturated Fat 2.2g
11%
Cholesterol 10mg
3%
Sodium 35mg
1%
Potassium 50mg
1%
Total Carbohydrates 11.5g
4%
Sugars 2.0g
Protein 1.9g

| Vitamin A 5% | • | Vitamin C 1% |
| Calcium 4% | • | Iron 3% |

Nutrition Grade B
* Based on a 2000 calorie diet
Nutrition Facts
Serving Size 53 g

Ingredients:

¼ cup risotto rice

3 tablespoons apricot puree

1-tablespoon butter

½ cup fresh milk

½ teaspoon cinnamon

Directions:

Preheat an oven to 300 °F then greases a baking dish with butter. Set aside.
Place the remaining butter together with apricot puree in a saucepan over very low heat.
When the butter is melted, stir well until incorporated.
Transfer the butter and apricot mixture to the prepared baking pan together with risotto rice.
Pour fresh milk into the pan then stir well and make sure that the rice is completely covered.
Bake for about an hour until the rice is light.
Once it is done, remove from the oven then let it cool for a few minutes.
Take about 2 scoops of the pudding and put in a small serving bowl.
Dust cinnamon on top and serve immediately.

Weight Watchers Smart Points Cookbook

Simple Apple Dip

SmartPoints: 12

Serving: 4

Nutrition Facts
Serving Size 101 g

Amount Per Serving
Calories 255
Calories from Fat 168
% Daily Value*
Total Fat 18.7g
29%
Saturated Fat 10.8g
54%
Trans Fat 0.0g
Cholesterol 0mg
0%
Sodium 156mg
6%
Potassium 295mg
8%
Total Carbohydrates 22.7g
8%
Dietary Fiber 3.9g
15%
Sugars 13.5g
Protein 3.6g

Vitamin A 0% • Vitamin C 16%
Calcium 1%   • Iron 11%
Nutrition Grade C+

* Based on a 2000 calorie diet

Ingredients:

2 apples

1 lime

½ cup chopped cashew

½ cup coconut milk

1-tablespoon coconut oil

½ teaspoon salt

Directions:

Cut apples into wedges then splash lime over the apples. Set aside.

Place cashew, coconut oil, and salt in a blender then pour coconut milk over the ingredients.

Blend on high speed until smooth and creamy.

Transfer the dip to a serving cup then serve with the apple wedges.

Serve and enjoy immediately.

Printed in Great Britain
by Amazon